Where Does a Letter Go?

Helena Ramsay

Illustrated by
Annabel Spenceley

CONTENTS

In this book we are going to follow the journey
of a letter from one side of the world to the other.

I'm writing to my pen-friend. She lives in Sydney, Australia.

The letter's journey is a complicated one. There are many stages to go through before it reaches its **destination**.

5

The cost of sending a letter by **airmail** depends on its weight. When you go to the post office, the clerk will weigh your letter. The clerk then calculates the postage costs and sells you stamps of the correct value.

My letter weighs 10 grams.

Airmail paper is lighter than ordinary writing paper. If you write a letter on airmail paper, it will cost less to send. It is important to use an airmail envelope, or to put an airmail sticker on your envelope. Blue airmail stickers make it easier to pick out the airmail when the letters are being sorted.

7

Once the letter has been stamped, it can be posted. This is the first stage in its long journey to Australia.

How long do letters stay in the post-box?

A postal worker usually empties the post-box two or three times each day. In big cities, **collections** take place even more often.

8

Post-boxes are made of thick metal to keep
the letters safe. At collection time, the postal
worker arrives in a van. He unlocks the box and
puts the letters into a sack.

The letters that the postal worker takes out of the box are all addressed to different places. Some of them, like our letter to Australia, are going overseas.

The job of the post office is to make sure that all these letters reach their different destinations.

How does the post office sort out all the letters?

When the postal worker has collected the letters, he takes them to the local **sorting office**. Here the letters are sorted according to where they are going.

While they are at the sorting office, the letters are handled by many people and several interesting machines.

Let's go and see what happens.

At the sorting office, the postal worker unloads the sacks of letters in the loading bay. The sacks are put on to trolleys and wheeled into the sorting area.

What's that machine?

In the sorting area, the sacks are emptied on to a **conveyor belt**, which carries the post into a machine called a culler facer canceller. The first task of this machine is to sort the letters from the packets. This is the culling stage.

The post goes into a large drum. As the drum
turns around, the letters slide out through slits.
The packets are too large to pass through the
slits. They leave the drum on a conveyor belt,
to be sorted by hand.

When the letters have left the drum, the machine
sorts them into different groups according to
their size.

What happens to the letters next?

The machine has a **sensing device** that enables it to find where the stamps are on the envelopes. It turns all the envelopes so that the stamps are in the top right-hand corner. This is called facing the letters.

The stamps are then cancelled so that they can't be used again. The machine does this by printing wavy lines across each one.

A **postmark** is printed on each letter. This gives the name of the town or city where the letter was sorted. It also shows the date and time the letter arrived at the sorting office.

15

The letters now go into another machine. This machine tries to recognize whatever is written on each envelope. It can sometimes even read handwriting! Its job is to read the addresses on the **inland** letters and print a code on them.

Inland letters that can't be read by the machine are coded by postal workers. Airmail letters pass through the machine without being coded.

The letters are unloaded from this machine, ready to go to a sorting machine. This will sort the letters into different piles, depending on their destinations.

When inland letters have been sorted, they are sent on to sorting offices all over the country. The postcode shows which sorting office they should go to.

Where does the airmail go to?

Airmail letters are separated from the inland mail and sent in sacks or trays to an international sorting office.

At the international sorting office, the letters are sorted according to the country they are going to.

After sorting, the letters are put into sacks. Each sack is labelled with the name of its destination.

My letter must be in this sack.

Our letter goes into the sack for Sydney.

21

The labels on the mail sacks have a **barcode** printed on them by a computer. Then the sacks leave the international sorting office to go to the airmail unit at the airport.

At the airport, the barcodes on the sacks are read by another computer.

When the sacks of letters have been logged by the computer, the workers in the airmail unit sort them for delivery to the different **airlines** at the airport. Each sack goes to the right airline for its destination.

23

The airline workers put the sacks into their own containers. It is easier to load one big container on to the aeroplane than lots of separate sacks.

Airmail letters usually travel in the hold of ordinary passenger aeroplanes.

24

The container with our letter is towed to an aeroplane and loaded into the hold on a lift. The aeroplane is ready to fly to Australia.

When the aeroplane arrives at Sydney Airport,
the containers holding mail and many other
things are unloaded from the hold.

The sacks
are taken
out of the
container
and driven
to a local sorting office. Here the letters are
sorted again, using the postcode marked at the
end of each address.

The postcode on my letter is NSW 2880.

NSW stands for the state of New South Wales, which is where Sydney is. The number 2 in the code stands for the state of New South Wales, too. The rest of the number relates to the exact location of the address in Sydney.

The letters are now sent to the delivery office in the area. Here they are sorted once more by the postal worker who will deliver them. She sorts the letters into the order in which she will walk up the street.

The postal worker is delivering our letter to Annette's house.

There's a letter for me from Great Britain!

It has taken only five days for the letter to arrive. Isn't that amazing?

29

Here are some of the different stages in our letter's journey to Australia. Can you remember what is happening at each stage?

1.

2.

3.

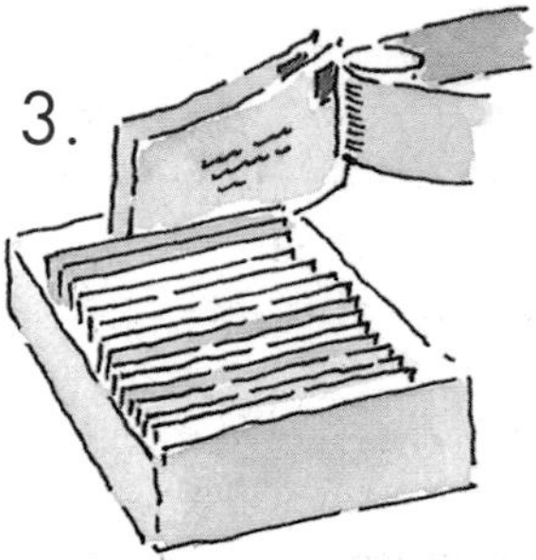

4.

5.

1. Letter is weighed 2. Letter is collected from post-box 3. Stamp is cancelled
4. Container is loaded on to aeroplane 5. Letter is delivered in Australia